"On behalf of the City of Orlando, I would like to congratulate you on your book...I am grateful for your dedication and active involvement in Central Florida and am thankful for the positive impact you are making in our community."
-- Buddy Dyer, **Mayor of Orlando, Florida**

"Tremendous! As an educator for over forty years, this book is spot on. This book should be required reading for all middle school students. Buy it and read it."
--Neal Gallagher, **PhD., retired engineering dean, and Princeton University graduate**

"What a powerful book! I wish this practical guide was available when I was in middle school. It's a must read for all middle school students."
-- Howard Schieferdecker, **Mayor of Maitland, FL**

"10 Steps is a practical guide for young people, with powerful lessons about excellence and positive aspirations. It is aimed at reaching them early enough that a change in direction can make a world of difference. Every middle school student should hear this message."
-- Alistair MacRae, **NYC-based cellist and teacher at Princeton University & The Brevard Music Center**

"A must read for all middle school parents and students. Samuel's story is sure to inspire any student to pursue a brighter future."
-- Faten Abdallah., **MA Ed. President of Socrates Preparatory School**

ACCOLADES

"Your voice is your source of power. Use it" p. 33. One great quote. Simple, and normally understated. This guide gives perfect examples of how to succeed...in middle school... and beyond! A must read."
-- Jeff Triplett, **Mayor of Sanford, Florida**

"What I love about new author Sam Konkol is that he's both personal and practical. His real-life stories are highly engaging. His advice is solid and success oriented. He's a young man to watch!"
– Don Jernigan, PhD, **President and CEO at Adventist Health Systems, the largest Protestant not-for-profit healthcare system in America**

"Superb advice from an obviously gifted young man! Sam Konkol's peers will find "10 Steps" to be extremely valuable as they navigate the waters of middle school... his stories will resonate and provide inspiration to a generation of future leaders."
-- Lieutenant General (retired) Mark Hertling, **US Army, CNN Analyst and Member of the President's Council on Fitness, Sports and Nutrition**

"If you're a teacher, you'll want your students to have this book. If you are a parent, you'll want your kids to follow Sam's advice. If you're a student, you'll want to read this book—multiple times!"
-- Lars Housmann, FACHE, **President and CEO of Florida Hospital, the largest admitting hospital in America**

10 STEPS
— TO A —
BRIGHTER FUTURE

A Middle School Guide

*The more that you read,
the more things you will know,
the more that you learn,
the more places you will go.*

- Dr. Seuss

10 STEPS
— TO A —
BRIGHTER FUTURE

A Middle School Guide

Samuel James Konkol

10 STEPS TO A BRIGHTER FUTURE:
A MIDDLE SCHOOL GUIDE
Copyright © 2015 Samuel James Konkol
Published by Collective Publishing, LLC
500 N. Maitland Ave. #313, Maitland, FL 32751

General Editor: Todd Chobotar
Copy Editor: Amanda Ruble
Production Editor: Collective Publishing, LLC
Project Coordinator: Amanda Ruble
Book Design: Collective Publishing, LLC

All rights reserved. No portion of this book may be reproduced, stored in a retrieval system, or transmitted in any form or by any means – electronic, mechanical, photocopy, recording, or any other – except for brief quotations in printed reviews, without the prior written permission of the publisher.

This book is a work of advice and opinion. Neither the authors nor the publisher is responsible for actions based on the content of this book. It is not the purpose of this book to include all information required to achieve a brighter future. The book should be used as a general guide and not as a totality of information on the subject.

ISBN-15: 978-0-9895144-3-9

Printed and bound in the United States of America

9 8 7 6 5 4 3 2 1

First Edition

www.SamuelKonkol.com

CONTENTS

Before You Begin:	How I Discovered My Passion	1
Step 1	Find Someone To Look Up To	9
Step 2	Start Caring	13
Step 3	Use Your Imagination	17
Step 4	Be Willing To Do Hard Stuff	21
Step 5	Stand Out	25
Step 6	Speak Up	31
Step 7	Read…Read…Read	35
Step 8	Learn To Love Math	39
Step 9	Make Learning Vocabulary Words Fun	45
Step 10	Pursue Mastery To Draw Out The Best In You	57
Your Turn Now:	Begin A Brighter Future	63

DEDICATION

*I would like to dedicate this book
to my middle school siblings:
Anna, Andrew, and Brantly*

FOREWORD

Rarely would one look for the "voice of experience" from one so young. But this is a delightful book of solid advice given by an unusually insightful teenager in a voice that will engage and motivate young teens to make the most of their middle school experience. I highly recommend it as a gift for new teens!

Sanford C. Shugart, PhD
President, Valencia College
Author, Leadership in
the Crucible of Work

"Ask not what your country can do for you, ask what you can do for your country."
- John F. Kennedy

BEFORE YOU BEGIN

How I Discovered My Passion

IN MIDDLE SCHOOL I WAS AN AVERAGE student. At first, I hated school and did just enough to get by. I had other interests that felt more important to me than school. Most of my friends and classmates were just like me—more interested in video games and television than in books and schoolwork.

If you are like most kids, when you don't like something, you don't spend much time trying to be successful at it. This described me. I avoided studying because I believed I was not—and could not be—good at school. However, during middle school, I fell in love with playing the cello and discovered music was something I could be good at. Because of my deep interest in music, my teacher told me one day about one of the best music schools in the world: The Juilliard School in New York City.

When I got out of school that day, I went home and read everything I could about Juilliard. I watched videos of Juilliard students, learned what the school had to offer, and found that some of the most famous musicians in the world had graduated from Juilliard. The more I discovered about Juilliard, the more interested in it I became. A few weeks later I told my mom and dad I would do a bazillion extra chores if I could go to New York and tour the school. My sister happened to be

When you don't like something, you don't spend much time trying to be successful at it.

going to New York a few months later with my dad on a college tour. Perfect! Maybe I wouldn't have to do the bazillion chores after all. I could hardly wait for the day to arrive.

When we arrived in New York City, we took a taxi straight to Juilliard and began the tour. The school was such a mystery to me. What would it look like? What were the kids like? Did I even stand a chance of getting in? Walking through the halls, I could hear students practicing, and as I peeked in on some classes, I imagined myself as one of those students. My mind swirled as I thought of having a chance to play for and learn from some of the best music teachers in the world.

I told my mom and dad I would do a bazillion extra chores.

That night my father asked me if we should get tickets to a student performance at Juilliard. I thought, are you kidding me? Of course! I wanted to see just how good these students were. Sitting in the concert hall waiting for the performance to begin, I kept looking at my phone, wondering why the seconds felt like years. My leg was bouncing up and down. I couldn't sit still. As I waited for what felt like a lifetime, I pictured myself on that stage doing exactly what those students were doing. I wasn't wondering anymore what Juilliard would be like; I was imagining myself as one of those students. After the concert, my dad asked, "So Sam, what did you think?" I remember looking at him and saying, "Everyone told me I could never get into Juilliard, but Dad, I think I can do this."

I wasn't wondering anymore. I was imagining myself as one of those students.

The students were really good, but not as good as I had feared they might be. It was at this life-changing moment the mystery of Juilliard was gone and I could see a bright future ahead of me. I had discovered my passion, and I now had a vision and a goal. Next stop: Juilliard.

A few months later, I was sitting in the hallway waiting for my sister's tutoring session to finish. I met her tutor and he invited me to shadow him by attending a school he taught at for a day to watch and observe. Even though I always thought I hated school, this one seemed different. I felt excited but also afraid—afraid I would embarrass myself in front of all those smart kids who snicker at the dumb answers kids give when they try to answer a question.

> *I had discovered my passion and I now had a vision and a goal.*

I wanted to shadow, but the fear of being laughed at wasn't worth it. I decided it would be easier to go to my regular school and do just enough to get by, so I canceled my shadow day. My parents insisted that I at least look at the school. I finally agreed to go. The night before my new shadow date, I couldn't sleep, and the next morning my stomach was in knots. I felt like I was going to throw up. What happened next? Well, I'll finish telling you my story a little later in the book.

First, here's what I want you to see. I felt bored, average, and unmotivated in school. Not because I was a bad student, but because I hadn't found the one thing that I was passionate to learn about. Once I found it, school took on new meaning to me. Finding something I was excited about gave me a vision for my future and goals I could set. It actually gave me energy for school.

What about you? Do you sometimes feel like an average or even a bad student? There's hope!

What about you? Do you sometimes feel unmotivated in school? Maybe you feel like an average student or even a bad student.

Maybe you've felt bored in school or wondered "What is the point of school?" If that's you, then great! There's hope. You have the right book in your hand! I want to share with you ten things I've learned about how to find something you're excited about, then how to take steps to turn that excitement into a bright vision for your future with goals that will help you get there. It's made a big difference for me, and it will for you too. So let's get started…

"The secret of getting ahead is getting started."
- Mark Twain

STEP 1

Find Someone To Look Up To

DO YOU HAVE SOMEONE YOU LOOK up to? If not, find someone. You can often find that person in a coach, an author, a teacher, or a relative.

I look up to Dr. Benjamin Carson. Dr. Carson is a retired brain surgeon who was raised by a single mother in one of the worst areas of Detroit, Michigan. Dr. Carson grew up very poor, and he hated it. Just like me, young Ben Carson struggled with low self-esteem. He believed he didn't have a bright future ahead of him. In fact, he thought he was the dumbest kid in his middle school class, and he was constantly bullied because of it. Kids laughed at and made fun of him for seeming so stupid.

Young Ben Carson loved watching television. Does this sound familiar? Watching television was so much more important to him than school. His mother was afraid that if he continued on this path, he would live his entire life being poor. According to Dr. Carson, his mother prayed, asking God for wisdom to show her what she could do to help her son avoid such a fate. The idea came to her to require her son to read two books a week and write a report on each one. Dr. Carson's mother realized a good education could provide the key to a bright future. She also made a rule that he was only allowed to

> *His mother was afraid that if he continued on this path, he would live his entire life being poor.*

watch two television shows a week—*after* completing his two book reports.

At the end of each week, his mother would collect the book reports and carefully review them, even though she only had a third-grade education. Slowly and carefully she went page by page, making marks and underlining different sections, even though she could barely read. When she was done, she would place a check mark at the top of the page and hand the paper back.

At first, Dr. Carson disliked being forced to read and write every day because none of the other kids in his neighborhood were required to do so, but after awhile, he grew to enjoy it. Reading books took him places he never imagined. A whole new world opened right before him, and soon he realized he could be smart. In fact, he soon rose to the top of his class.

Because of Dr. Carson's decision to focus on school, he graduated from high school with the highest honors, attended Yale University, then the University of Michigan Medical School, and was later appointed the head of Johns Hopkins Children's Center at the young age of thirty-three.

I look up to Dr. Carson because he showed me how to overcome low self-esteem. When I looked at the challenges he faced as a middle school student, I came to realize that if Dr. Carson could overcome his obstacles, I could overcome mine, and you can too!

BOTTOM LINE

Find someone to look up to. Discover what they did to overcome their problems to succeed. Then, follow their example. Use their story to inspire you!

STEP 2

Start Caring

YOU MAY BE ASKING YOURSELF, "Why should I care? After all, I am only in middle school, so I have plenty of time to be thinking about my future." You may have a point, but sometime, perhaps before you realize it, you will need to make decisions about your future. Your parents, your teachers, your friends—they cannot make these decisions for you. You must make them. Many kids think they can start caring tomorrow; then tomorrow comes and goes, and a decision about their future is never made.

Hey...I am not saying that you have to give up your life of fun or stop doing the things that you enjoy, like playing sports, listening to music, or hanging out with your friends. I *am* pointing out, however, that high school is just around the corner, and the longer you wait to make a decision about your brighter future, the more opportunities you will miss.

At one time it was cool to be silly or dumb in class. This is no longer true. Now it is cool to be smart, and *the opportunity to make a difference in your future is right in front of you.* Remember Dr. Carson? By his own admission, he thought he was the dumbest student in his class. But today he has grown to be known as one of the leading figures in America. Dr. Carson was in middle school when he got serious about school and his future. He could've refused to read, but where do you think he would be today if he had continued to watch all of that television? I would guess that he never would have been a brain surgeon, written so many books, saved so many lives, and been an inspiration to millions of people.

Now I am the first to admit when I was younger, school wasn't my favorite thing. But I have since discovered that middle school is the perfect time to start caring. In fact, it's never too soon to start caring! Because when you start to care about your future, you'll begin to take the steps you need to succeed. You'll start dreaming about your future. You'll start looking for the thing you can study and be passionate about. You'll get a clear vision of your future and what goals to set. You'll find someone to look up to who

> When you start to care about your future, you'll begin to take the steps you need to succeed.

inspires you. And you may even want to read books (like this one) that can help you succeed.

BOTTOM LINE

If you dare to care, you'll grow more aware and start to prepare for your future success.

STEP 3

Use Your Imagination

I HAD A REALLY COOL OPPORTUNITY TO meet with a professor at a top university, and he shared something with me that I would like to pass along to you. After I asked for his advice on a project, he told me something I totally didn't expect. He said, "Use your imagination. Don't be limited by obstacles. Allow your mind to imagine what is possible, and if you do, you may very well be surprised where your idea takes you."

Why did this advice surprise me? Because I'm so used to teachers having all the right answers. Often it feels like success in school simply comes from memorizing facts and figures and remembering them for quizzes and tests. Do you ever feel that way too?

Well, here was a very wise professor telling me to use my imagination. To not just try and find "the one right answer" but to imagine the possibilities and see where it took me. Just like most kids, I love to use my imagination!

So picture this. Imagine what your life can be like if you dream beyond what you believe is possible. Close your eyes for just one moment and dream about something so big that it not only seems impossible to achieve, but others might think you have completely

Imagine what your life can be like if you dream big dreams beyond what you believe is possible.

lost your mind. Go ahead, close your eyes. Don't skip this important step. Once you have identified this dream beyond the stars, don't let yourself think of the reasons this dream might seem impossible. Most dreams are crushed because we tell ourselves all of the reasons why we can't do something.

Imagine what life would be like if Martin Luther King didn't dream a big dream, or President John F. Kennedy didn't dream about landing a man on the moon, or Steve Jobs didn't dream it was possible to create an iPhone.

You, too, have an imagination and are capable of dreaming big dreams. Don't allow your mind to tell you that you can't.

BOTTOM LINE

Be a dreamer. Use your imagination to dream a big dream of your future.

"Everything you can image is real."

\- Pablo Picasso

Step 4

Be Willing To Do Hard Stuff

TAKE IT FROM SOMEONE WHO learned the hard way. Don't take an easy math class to get an easy "A" when you have the ability to take a math class that prepares you for high school and beyond. I know what you are thinking: this sounds like a lot of work. But trust me, you won't regret it.

Consider my experience. There I was, sitting, as usual, smack-dab in the back row in seventh grade, drawing cartoon characters on my notepad, doing just enough not to be noticed by my teachers, believing I had plenty of time to get my act together. After all, high school was still nearly two years away, and I could start focusing on my studies once I began the ninth grade, if not later. What I eventually learned, though, was that settling for the standard math class I took in seventh grade didn't prepare me for the math classes I needed to take in high school. When I got to high school, I ended up having to take geometry over the summer to get back on track. Math during the summer? What a bummer!

I realized my mistake one night at dinner when my older sister was telling my family about her college tours. When she first began talking, I immediately zoned out. All I heard was school, school, school. Over and over she kept saying how each and every college information session began with the same words: "The first and most important thing we look for is the difficulty of the classes you chose to take in high school and the grades you earned in them."

What she said made me sit up and listen. "Hey!" I said. "Wait a minute? Do you mean all of the straight A's I get in PE, band, and art don't matter that much?"

My sister responded, "Colleges mostly look at the top five core classes—math, science, history, English, and foreign language. Sam, when you get to high school you will have the option of taking different levels of difficulty in each of these subjects. They include standard, honors,

Advanced Placement (AP), or International Baccalaureate (IB). It is important to show colleges that you took the most difficult classes you could and got good grades in them."

This is when I realized I was behind. If I wanted to attend a good college, I would need to get to work preparing for the classes to come!

Best-selling author T. Harv Eker says, "If you are willing to do only what is easy, life will be hard. But if you are willing to do what is hard, life will be easy."

So don't take the easy way out. Harder classes may be just what you need to get ahead faster and be better prepared for your bright future!

BOTTOM LINE

*Be willing to do what is hard,
so later your life will be easier.*

STEP 5

Stand Out

HAVE YOU EVER EXPERIENCED A time when you were so embarrassed that you felt your face turn red, and you wanted to hide under your chair?

Well, this happened to me.

One day I asked my dad if I could meet with a college guidance counselor so I could better understand how to get into a good college. I met the guidance counselor in his office. He told me about all of the good things college had to offer. For the next twenty minutes he explained the entire process to me; then he leaned back in his chair and said, "So Sam, tell me something about yourself." I proudly responded, "Well, I have all A's and B's this semester." For the next five seconds (which felt like forever!) he stared blankly at me, and I realized he expected more of an answer. I felt hot and knew my face probably had turned red as a tomato, and that's when I crawled under my chair (well, not really!). I later realized I should have been able to share more about myself than just about getting good grades.

> *I later realized I should have been able to share more about myself than just about getting good grades.*

He could sense that I was feeling uncomfortable, so he shared that it would take way more than just good grades to get into a good college. To get into a good college I would have to do some things that would make me stand out. He suggested becoming the captain of my soccer team or a member of the student council and to look for leadership opportunities. He finished by saying, "Keep in mind, even perfect grades and lots of involvement in activities won't guarantee that you'll get into a top college, but at least these things will put you on the right path."

Ideas For Extracurricular Activities You Can Do To Make You Stand Out:

Community Service – When you do something to help others and don't expect to get anything in return, it shows what a caring, responsible person you are. So find a way to volunteer. You can check with nursing homes, soup kitchens, libraries, day care facilities, The Humane Society, The Red Cross, or homeless shelters. Always get permission from your parents first, of course.

Music or Arts – Participating in music, drama, or some other form of the arts shows that you have discipline and determination. Why not learn a new instrument, learn to dance, or take some extracurricular classes in painting or drawing? Consider joining the school band, choir, or orchestra. Try out for school or community theater plays. Take a class in photography, design, or art. If your school doesn't have a class like this, try a local community center.

Athletics – Playing a sport is great exercise and can take a lot of hard work and dedication. This is something colleges like to see. Why not look into your school sports program or local community leagues? You could look at some team sports like soccer, volleyball, baseball, softball, basketball, badminton, football, lacrosse, cheerleading, hockey, and gymnastics. You could look at some more individual sports like track & field, cross-country, golf, wrestling, martial arts, dance, swimming, diving, and tennis.

Clubs or Associations – You might really enjoy being part of a club, group, or association that can also help you prepare for college. Here are some ideas: foreign language club, drama club, the debate team, math club, book club, chess team, Christian fellowship club, student government, business club, robotics club, National Honor Society, science olympiad, cooking club, computer programming club, key club, school newspaper, or yearbook. The main thing is to find something you can dedicate your time and energy to and do it! If you don't have the kind of club in your area that you'd like to join, then maybe you should start it!

One last thing…

Don't go overboard. If you try to do TOO many activities in the hope of impressing a college admission counselor, you could wear yourself out (and your parents!) and not be very good at anything. Pick just a couple of things you can do well at and have fun doing. This is more impressive than dealing with burnout.

BOTTOM LINE

Don't think that good grades alone will guarantee you a brighter future.

Step 6

Speak Up

How many times have you known the right answer in class but didn't speak up because you were afraid your classmates might laugh if you were wrong?

When I was in elementary school, my classmates and I were required to participate in a speaking contest. Like most of the kids in my class, I was scared.

I thought, *Does my teacher really think I am going to stand up and speak in front of the class? No way!*

I brought the assignment home, and my parents worked with me on getting the words just right. Every night for what seemed like forever I would have to stand up in the living room and say, "Hi, my name is Sam Konkol, and today I want to share with you…" blah blah blah.

I would often hope that my parents would forget to ask me to practice, but they never did, and eventually my efforts paid off.

The day came when I had to stand in front of the class and give my speech. I was trembling nervously, but when I began to speak, everyone was quiet—no one said a word, and no one laughed at me. As I continued speaking I gained more and more confidence, and when I was done everyone stood up and applauded. I had done it! I felt great being able to speak without being afraid.

Did you know the most common fear

Your voice is your source of power. Use it!

people have is public speaking? Yes, they fear it more than snakes, spiders, or heights. If this sounds like you, don't be ashamed. The sooner you can overcome your fear, the better prepared you will be when you are required to speak in public. In the future, you can join a debate club or take a class in speech or public speaking. Always be on the lookout for chances to speak— either inside or outside of the classroom.

> *The sooner you can overcome your fear, the better prepared you will be when you are required to speak in public.*

Your voice is your source of power. Use it.

Since that day, I have gained confidence in speaking, not only in class, but out of class as well. Sure, it's normal to be nervous before you stand up to speak—nearly everyone is—but don't let that slow you down.

Recently I had the opportunity to shadow a music class at a top university. I quietly walked in the classroom and sat down at an empty desk. After his lecture, the professor asked a question and then looked for a volunteer to answer it. I raised my hand. After scanning the room, he called on me, "Yes, please share with the class what the word 'cadence' means."

I answered confidently. He seemed impressed, knowing that I was a high school student shadowing his class. Don't just speak up in school—do it everywhere! You may be surprised where your confidence can take you.

BOTTOM LINE

Your ability to confidently speak up will contribute to your brighter future.

STEP 7

Read…Read…Read

I KNOW YOU MIGHT BE TEMPTED TO skip this chapter…but hang on! For most of my life, I didn't enjoy reading. My parents told me and my siblings a million times that life would be easier if we could read well. Blah, blah, blah. I was tired of hearing it. (I hope my parents aren't reading this.)

This is precisely why all of our teachers encourage us to improve our reading skills. My father requires my siblings to read for ninety minutes every day, summers included! No one in our home (except my mom) is allowed to watch television until we have finished reading. Whenever we drive past a bookstore or library, my dad asks if we want to get some new books to read. At first, we kids would just roll our eyes in the backseat. But we had to be careful our parents weren't looking in the rearview mirror! However, the more we read, the wider our interests became. Doctor Ben Carson's world came alive when he explored books, and your world will too!

When you read and explore books, your world comes alive!

Personally, I have made it a habit to have a book with me wherever I go. Yes, every-where...even to the movies! (Okay, not really). Even if I only have a few minutes to read, having a book at my side helps me read regularly. Ever since I developed the habit of carrying a book, I read a lot more than I used to.

Would you be interested in a way to earn money from your parents and help make them happy with you in the process? Ask them if they would be willing to pay you one dollar for every book that you read, starting today.

Just think: if you read a million books, you can become a millionaire.

If you read a billion books, you can become a billionaire.

If you read a trillion books…well, you get the idea.

Think of reading as your ticket to a brighter future. Reading can be fun, especially when you read about topics that are interesting to you. The more you read, the better reader you will become.

BOTTOM LINE

Make it a habit to always have a book with you to read, even if it's only for a few minutes at a time.

"Life is like riding a bicycle. To keep your balance, you must keep moving."

— Albert Einstein

Step 8

Learn to Love Math

MATH WAS ALWAYS ONE OF MY worst subjects. Ever since the third grade, math has been a real challenge for me. Every year, the first weeks of my new math class would start out well, but a few weeks later I would fall behind the other kids, and for the rest of the year I would struggle. Every year math class was like a bad dream I kept having over and over.

Then one day everything changed for me. Someone suggested that I approach math the same way I approached playing the cello.

The cello is now easy for me to play, but it wasn't always easy. When I first started playing the cello, it was hard…I mean really hard! My cello squeaked and squawked and made tons of really weird sounds. My siblings begged me to stop playing because they got tired of listening to the neighborhood dogs howl every time I played. It took a long time for me to be able to perfectly play five notes in a row. I would practice those same five notes over and over again…sometimes for hours at a time.

My cello squeaked and squawked and made tons of really weird sounds.

Was it frustrating? You bet it was!

Was it boring at times? Absolutely!

Did I try to convince myself that the five notes were good enough? Yes, hundreds of times.

Did I feel like quitting?

More times than I can count.

But when I finally played those five notes perfectly three times in a row…I had a completely different attitude. I said to myself, give me five more notes and I will conquer them as well.

> *I said to myself, give me five more notes and I will conquer them as well.*

And then five more…then five more…and soon I was able to play with confidence note after note.

Why? Because every future set of notes relies on the ability to know the previous ones. Math works the same way. Each math concept is dependent on understanding the previous one. I learned to conquer each concept thoroughly before advancing to the next one.

Sometimes a math problem comes easily, other times it takes a few more minutes, and other times it may take an hour or more. But I learned that there are no shortcuts to learning math or to playing the cello. I can tell you firsthand, the extra time is well worth it.

For some, this may mean going back and relearning multiplication tables; after all, math will be much more challenging if you have to count on your fingers every time you want to figure out 9 × 8. For others, it may mean going back a year or two and working through an entire math book to fully understand math concepts. Others may require tutoring. In my case, I decided to take a geometry course over the summer.

> *In my case, I decided to take a geometry course over the summer.*

Math is such a huge part of our daily lives that it should never be taken for granted. All of the major colleges test your understanding of math, but you also need it in your everyday life. Do not make the mistake I made in just learning enough to get by. Learn to love math, because once you do, math will become easy and you may develop a desire to learn more of it. Take it from someone who avoided math at all costs but now looks forward to math and intends to complete Calculus II before graduating from high school.

BOTTOM LINE

Learn to love math, and you will not regret it.

"Do not go where the path may lead, go instead where there is no path and leave a trail."

- Ralph Waldo Emerson

STEP 9

Make Learning Vocabulary Words Fun

How in the world could learning vocabulary words be fun? Let me tell you. While on a college tour, my family and I were snowed in and stranded in a hotel room for nearly three days. My father didn't want to waste one precious moment on our college trip, so he had the bright idea of making my siblings and me learn vocabulary words for the SAT, a college entrance exam. Hour after hour, we had to tell him the definitions of five hundred words. The first few hours were okay, but after nearly three days of this we couldn't stand it anymore.

We begged him to stop.

Was it torture? Yes!

Was it cruel? Yes!

I made a promise to myself that when I became a father, I would never do this to my children. It felt like we learned enough vocabulary words for a lifetime. Oh, did I mention that we had to eat all of our meals from a gas station across the street from our hotel because all other businesses were closed due to the snowstorm? Guess what? We had to do vocabulary words while we ate our gas station junk food. NOT FUN!

Oh, did I mention that we had to eat all of our meals from a gas station across the street from our hotel because all other business were closed due to the snowstorm?

Of course, looking back on that experience now makes me laugh. I didn't know it at the time, but it was the beginning of my love for vocabulary. After that weekend of misery, I began to notice those words in my everyday life. When I would listen to a sermon in church, I would recognize at least one—and sometimes as many as three or four—vocabulary words. As I watched the news, more and more of these vocabulary words would come to life. As I continued to read, these new words seemed to jump off the page.

Learning vocabulary words has now become a fun game in our family. We seldom take a family car ride without practicing many new vocabulary words. Even my nine-year-old brother joins in. We compete to see who can first name the definition of a vocabulary word.

At first I learned only one hundred words. Then I learned five hundred. Now my goal before graduating from high school is to know three thousand of the most common college test vocabulary words. I am over halfway there and am enjoying the challenge; you can too! What began as a chore has turned into a lot of fun!

You can find SAT vocabulary words by doing a simple Google search. It's easy, it's fun, and your reading will become much more meaningful.

BOTTOM LINE

Growing your vocabulary can be fun and will make reading more meaningful. Get started today!

100 Vocabulary Words You Should Know
(To Get You Going)

1. **abbreviate** -- to shorten, abridge

2. **abstinence** -- the act of refraining from pleasurable activity, i.e., eating or drinking

3. **adulation** -- high praise

4. **adversity** -- misfortune, an unfavorable turn of events

5. **aesthetic** -- pertaining to beauty or the arts

6. **amicable** -- friendly, agreeable

7. **anachronistic** -- out-of-date, not attributed to the correct historical period

8. **anecdote** -- short, usually funny account of an event

9. **anonymous** -- nameless, without a disclosed identity

10. **antagonist** -- foe, opponent, adversary

11. **arid** -- extremely dry or deathly boring

12. **assiduous** -- persistent, hard working

13. **asylum** -- sanctuary, shelter, place of refuge

14. **benevolent** -- friendly and helpful

15. **camaraderie** -- trust, sociability among friends

16. **censure** -- to criticize harshly

17. **circuitous** -- indirect, taking the longest route

18. **clairvoyant** -- exceptionally insightful, able to foresee the future

19. **collaborate** -- to cooperate, work together

20. **compassion** -- sympathy, helpfulness, or mercy

21. **compromise** -- to settle a dispute by terms agreeable to both sides

22. **condescending** -- possessing an attitude of superiority, patronizing

23. **conditional** -- depending on a condition, e.g., in a contract

24. **conformist** -- person who complies with accepted rules and customs

25. **congregation** -- a crowd of people, an assembly

26. **convergence** -- the state of separate elements joining or coming together

27. **deleterious** -- harmful, destructive, detrimental

28. **demagogue** -- leader, rabble-rouser, appealing to emotion or prejudice

29. **digression** -- the act of turning aside, straying from the main point

30. **diligent** -- careful and hardworking

31. **discredit** -- to harm the reputation of, dishonor, or disgrace

32. **disdain** -- to regard with scorn or contempt

33. **divergent** -- separating, moving in different directions from a particular point

34. **empathy** -- identification with the feelings of others

35. **emulate** -- to imitate, follow an example

36. **enervating** -- weakening, tiring

37. **enhance** -- to improve, bring to a greater level of intensity

38. **ephemeral** -- momentary, transient, fleeting

39. **evanescent** -- quickly fading, short-lived, esp. an image

40. **exasperation** -- irritation, frustration

41. **exemplary** -- outstanding, an example to others

42. **extenuating** -- excusing, lessening the seriousness of guilt or crime

43. **florid** -- red-colored, flushed; gaudy, ornate

44. **fortuitous** -- happening by luck, fortunate

45. **frugal** -- thrifty, cheap

46. **hackneyed** -- clichéd, worn out by overuse

47. **haughty** -- arrogant and condescending

48. **hedonist** -- person who pursues pleasure as a goal

49. **hypothesis** -- assumption, theory requiring proof

50. **impetuous** -- rash, impulsive, acting without thinking

51. **impute** -- to attribute an action to a particular person or group

52. **incompatible** -- opposed in nature, not able to live or work together

53. **inconsequential** -- unimportant, trivial

54. **inevitable** -- certain, unavoidable

55. **integrity** -- decency, honesty, wholeness

56. **intrepid** -- fearless, adventurous

57. **intuitive** -- instinctive, untaught

58. **jubilation** -- joy, celebration, exultation

59. **lobbyist** -- person who seeks to influence political events

60. **longevity** -- long life

61. **mundane** -- ordinary, commonplace

62. **nonchalant** -- calm, casual, seeming unexcited

63. **novice** -- apprentice, beginner

64. **opulent** -- wealthy

65. **orator** -- lecturer, speaker

66. **ostentatious** -- showy, displaying wealth

67. **parched** -- dried up, shriveled

68. **perfidious** -- faithless, disloyal, untrustworthy

69. **precocious** -- unusually advanced or talented at an early age

70. **pretentious** -- pretending to be important, intelligent, or cultured

71. **procrastinate** -- to unnecessarily delay, postpone, put off

72. **prosaic** -- relating to prose; dull, commonplace

73. **prosperity** -- wealth or success

74. **provocative** -- tending to provoke a response, e.g., anger or disagreement

75. **prudent** -- careful, cautious

76. **querulous** -- complaining, irritable

77. **rancorous** -- bitter, hateful

78. **reclusive** -- preferring to live in isolation

79. **reconciliation** -- the act of agreement after a quarrel, the resolution of a dispute

80. **renovation** -- repair, making something new again

81. **resilient** -- quick to recover, bounce back

82. **restrained** -- controlled, repressed, restricted

83. **reverence** -- worship, profound respect

84. **sagacity** -- wisdom

85. **scrutinize** -- to observe carefully

86. **spontaneity** -- impulsive action, unplanned events

87. **spurious** -- lacking authenticity, false

88. **submissive** -- tending to meekness, to submit to the will of others

89. **substantiate** -- to verify, confirm, provide supporting evidence

90. **subtle** -- hard to detect or describe; perceptive

91. **superficial** -- shallow, lacking in depth

92. **superfluous** -- extra, more than enough, redundant

93. **suppress** -- to end an activity, e.g., to prevent the dissemination of information

94. **surreptitious** -- secret, stealthy

95. **tactful** -- considerate, skillful in acting to avoid offense to others

96. **tenacious** -- determined, keeping a firm grip on

97. **transient** -- temporary, short-lived, fleeting

98. **venerable** -- respected because of age

99. **vindicate** -- to clear from blame or suspicion

100. **wary** -- careful, cautious

"Believe you can and you're halfway there."
- Theodore Roosevelt

STEP 10

Pursue Mastery To Draw Out The Best In You

WHAT IS "MASTERY"? SIMPLY put, mastery is getting really good at something. Mastery involves getting so good at a certain thing that you fully understand it.

Let's say you want to be a master cellist. You would have to understand all of the small details, how the cello relates to you, and how to understand music in a new and more profound way. Some people say mastery requires ten thousand hours of practice. However, don't believe that mastery is the ten thousand hours alone.

For me, mastery is not about the goal but about the process of getting there. As an aspiring cellist, for instance, I am not consumed with the end result after investing ten thousand hours of practicing the cello. Instead, I am inspired by the type of person I will become as a result of practicing long before most people get up in the morning and long after most people go to bed. Once you master something, mastery itself becomes a part of you. Some would say it is a skill. I would say, it is an identity.

> Once you master something, mastery itself becomes a part of you.

The process of mastery for me includes playing a single bar of Mozart so slowly and precisely that someone walking by would not recognize it as Mozart. By playing this piece over and over until every note is precise and perfect, and by practicing so intensely, after two hours of practice I am completely exhausted.

Will I ever become a performing cellist? Only time will tell. Truthfully, I do not worry about becoming a world-class performer. I just focus on being the best cellist I can be. Whether I end up a performing cellist, a scientific researcher, or a foreign ambassador, I know I will have taken the path that enables me to be my best. The process of mastering anything is worthwhile, even if that particular skill ends up not being at the center of your life. Mastering one thing makes you the kind of person who will do well at other things.

Is there something that you want to be the

best at? Then go for it. Don't let anyone discourage you or tell you why you can't. Pursue mastery, not as an end game, but rather as a means to draw out the best in you.

After understanding the definition of mastery, you might be wondering how you can achieve mastery: start by searching for "pockets of time" to begin your ten thousand hours of practice. A pocket of time is any amount of time you can focus on doing something. For example, car rides are the perfect example of pockets of time. I used to spend a car ride either playing on my phone or looking out the window, but when I realized that the twenty-minute car ride to school could be spent focusing on becoming a master of something, I began using most car rides to work on something beneficial to my future.

> *A pocket of time is any amount of time you can focus on doing something.*

The next step you can do to achieve mastery is practice, but not in the traditional sense. The type of practice that will contribute to your journey to mastery is what I have come to know as "deep practice." Deep practice is focused or as I mentioned earlier, playing a bar of Mozart so slowly and precisely that no one would be able to recognize it. Deep practice is committed, precise, and normally not too glamorous. Plan out your sessions of deep practice and commit to sticking to the plan you have created.

Finally, if you want to pursue true mastery, search endlessly for great teachers that can contribute to your journey and help make you a master. I have found that when I am around people that are better than me, I become better.

BOTTOM LINE

Pursue mastery—not for the end result, but for who you become in the process.

"Whatever you are, be a good one."
- Abraham Lincoln

Your Turn Now

Begin A Brighter Future

JUST A SHORT TIME AGO, I WAS IN middle school just like you. I was already giving up and didn't see a bright future ahead of me. I was allowing my fear of failure to limit my future. Having doubts and worries is completely normal. We all have them. Too often we let our concerns and worries be the excuses for why we can't reach great heights and accomplish our goals.

Do you remember at the beginning of the book when I told you that I had shadowed at a new school? I promised I would finish that story. Well, as you may remember…I wanted to shadow, but the fear of being laughed at wasn't worth it. I decided it would be be easier to go to my regular school and do just enough to get by, so I cancelled my shadow day. My parents insisted that I at least look at the school. After careful consideration I finally agreed to go. The night before my shadow date, I couldn't sleep, and the next morning my stomach was in knots. I felt like I was going to throw up.

When my parents picked me up at the end of the day, I couldn't wait to tell them what had happened. When I got in the car, I could not stop talking. I told my parents what an incredible, awesome, fantastic day I'd had and that this was the school I wanted to attend. I felt that I could finally be good at a school that would help me succeed. No one laughed at me. No one poked fun at me.

I felt that I could finally be good at a school that would help me succeed.

The teachers showed a real interest in me and they believed in me. I realized that no matter what my previous academics looked like, I could have a bright future.

School and learning came alive. I realized the possibilities and opportunities right in front of me! For the first time in my life I didn't feel average in school. I no longer worried about what other kids thought because I didn't feel afraid of failing or being judged. I realized that school and learning could help me build a brighter future.

> *I no longer worried about what other kids thought because I didn't feel afraid of failing.*

Yes, attending a different school was helpful, but as I look back on the experience I realize it wasn't the only thing that helped change my view of school. It was a combination of many things along the way that helped me realize a brighter future.

Part of the reason I wrote this book is to help you SUCCEED and DREAM BIG! The other reason I wrote it is to help myself SUCCEED and DREAM BIG! I am on this journey, just like you are. My hope is that this book will inspire you to plan for a brighter future. Too often, students decide to just drift through their days, unconcerned about their future. You will eventually hear all of this same advice as you prepare for college, but by that time it may be too late to get started.

DON'T wait until your high school years to plan for a brighter future; your brighter future starts now. Let's go!

My hope is that this book will inspire you to plan for a brighter future.

Samuel Konkol

About The Author

Samuel Konkol is a sixteen-year-old aspiring cellist, entrepreneur, cello instructor, speaker, and the author of the book *"10 Steps to a Brighter Future — A Middle School Guide."* There are over 55,000+ public middle school students in Central Florida, and each week, Samuel speaks to them about the benefits of planning for their brighter future. He launched a Kickstarter campaign and raised $12,000 to underwrite the printing costs of the next 10,000 copies of his book in order to provide a free copy to every middle school student he speaks to. Samuel created a Cello Scholarship Program for elementary students and also raised the funds to purchase six cellos, one for each scholarship recipient. He teaches them group cello lessons on a weekly basis. Samuel is currently collaborating with

About The Author

other high school students to create other Strings Scholarship Programs in elementary schools throughout Central Florida. Samuel provides private cello lessons to students but offers scholarships for those who are unable to pay for private lessons. At age 16, Samuel made his debut at Carnegie Hall in New York City. He placed first in the state cello competition and is in the Precollege Cello Program at Stetson University. Samuel is also the founder of "Plato Tutoring," an afterschool tutoring program where he recruits high school students to provide free tutoring services for elementary students. Samuel comes from a family of ten children and resides in Maitland, Florida.

Konkol Family Photo

The Cello Scholarship Program

Samuel with His Cello

ORDER BULK COPIES

Samuel Konkol
500 N. Maitland Ave #313
Maitland, FL 32751

Phone: 407.913.9974

Email: SamuelJamesKonkol@gmail.com

Website: www.SamuelKonkol.com

1-9 copies $12.95 each

10-25 copies $10.95 each

26-100 copies $9.95 each

101-500 copies $7.95 each

FREE postage and handling on all orders.

Hear More From Samuel Konkol

If you would like to invite Samuel Konkol to speak to your group, please contact Samuel at the address below. Please include dates, times, and location in your request.

Samuel Konkol
500 N. Maitland Ave #313
Maitland, FL 32751

Phone: 407.913.9974
Email: SamuelJamesKonkol@gmail.com
Website: www.SamuelKonkol.com

Samuel Speaks on Many Topics, Including:

- 10 Steps to a Brighter Future
- How to Discover Your Passion in Life
- How to create a Musical Scholarship Program
- How to succeed at a competitive music camp
- What it is like to grow up as one of ten siblings
- How to not live in the shadow of your older sibling(s)